HOW TO HIT A GOLF BALL

From Any Sort of Lie

"Slammin' Sam" Snead

I0202381

Edited by
Mark Cox

COACHWHIP PUBLICATIONS

Greenville, Ohio

How to Hit a Golf Ball From Any Sort of Lie, by Sam Snead
Copyright © 2013 Coachwhip Publications
Front cover: Golf Course © Cheung Chi Man
No claims made on public domain material.
First published 1950.

ISBN 1-61646-203-5
ISBN-13 978-1-61646-203-1

CoachwhipBooks.com

FOREWORD

Throughout my years of tournament golf the one question most repeatedly asked of me, and of my fellow players, has been "What club did you use?" When the spectators see the ball shoot up out of any kind of a lie, good, fair or terrible, they always want to know what club did the job.

Well, that's what this little book is for. I have told, in the following pages, when and how I use each club. I haven't said a great deal about form—that's pretty well covered in my book How to Play Golf— because correct form is something it generally takes a little time to master. But by using the right club for each shot, under all the varying conditions found on any golf course, you at least give yourself a good chance to get the ball up in the air, on its way to the hole.

Almost from the moment that Mr. L. B. Icely gave me my start in competitive golf, I realized that every round of golf furnished a new challenge in itself. Practically no two holes are played alike. Few shots are played under identical conditions.

By applying the information I've tried to give— together with sound fundamentals as taught by your own pro, and sufficient practice—I sincerely believe your golf game will show progressive improvement.

SAM SNEAD

Sam Snead's classic summary of how he plays golf, in his own lexicon of the hills, is "Ah plays the shots the most simplest way ah knows how." That historic remark, made at the instruction clinic of a Professional Golfers Association annual meeting, is the honest explanation of the game of the most gifted golfer any of us have ever seen. Plenty of times his colleagues in the star realm of professional golf have volunteered to Sam some advice on delicate details but he just thanks them and walks along, contented to be playing the way he does. And that way is good enough for any of us.

Since Sam's been teaching I've seen that he applies to teaching as well as playing the "the most simplest way" and it has been effective for a multitude of muscle-bound elders and the limber younger people. Professional golfers have made astonishing progress in the difficult task of teaching golf, especially to the athletically inept. Sam has done his good share in contributing to this advance with his work in making the directions so simple muscles can understand them.

Snead doesn't try to delude with the vision of being able to play as he does for he is a fellow of rare physical qualifications. But he does a great job of showing the simple way of making the most of one's own qualifications and in this book gives enough advice on how to hit a golf ball so it will save embarrassment and blushes when you look at your card. The advice probably will save you some money, too, if you play with the same type of delightful burglars with whom I spend sunny hours when I should be throwing away my life in work.

HERB GRAFFIS
Editor, Golfing and Golfdom.

CONTENTS

HOW TO GRIP A GOLF CLUB

In view of the fact that you start out every golf shot by gripping the club, it seems only logical that this book should begin with the grip.

Personally, I use a glove (no fingers) which covers the palm of my left hand and helps me grip the club firmly. I am also partial to the "Reminder Grip" on my clubs which has a flat side to fit against the left hand and automatically guides the left hand into proper position.

The grip used is basically the same for hitting all wood and iron shots. There is a slight difference in the putting grip which will be discussed in the section on putting later in the book.

This is the grip I use

By far the most popular grip among golfers is the overlapping grip, introduced by Harry Vardon many years ago. I form the grip by soling the wood flat on the ground and letting the leather of the club shaft lie diagonally across my left hand. When I close my fingers to grip the shaft, the thumb of the left hand runs down the outside of the shaft. The V formed by thumb and forefinger should point over the right shoulder.

1

I grip the shaft with the fingers of my right hand so the palm of that hand covers the thumb of the left. The little finger of the right hand overlaps the first finger of the left, and the V formed by the thumb and forefinger of the right hand also points over the right shoulder.

This grip may feel awkward at first, but practice will familiarize you with it. It is considered the finest grip for control of the club and increased power for the majority of golfers.

THE STANCE

Your stance on every shot will vary according to whether you are using a wood or an iron, and what purpose you intend the shot to fulfill. The stance for each shot will be dealt with as the various shots are discussed.

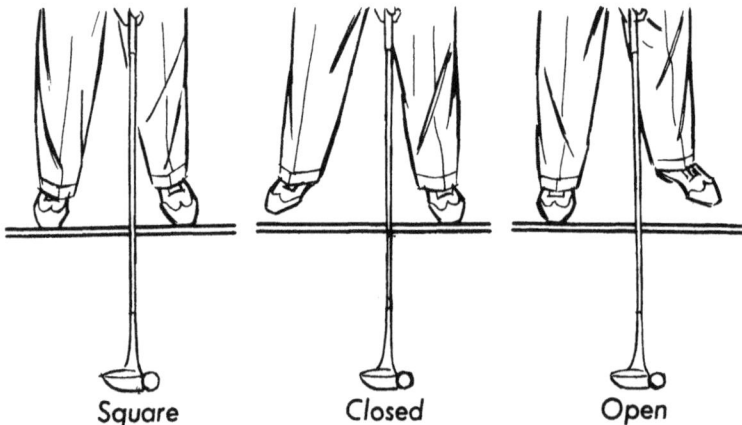

Square   Closed   Open

However, I will define the three basic stances—square, open and closed. The square stance is one in which both feet are square to the intended line of flight.

The open stance is one in which the left foot is drawn farther back from the intended line of flight than the right foot, turning the body slightly toward your objective.

The closed stance is just the opposite—the right foot is farther from the line of flight than the left foot.

THE WOODS ARE THE CLUBS
FOR DISTANCE

Wood shots have always been favorites of mine, but I know many golfers who dread the thought of hitting a wood.

Really, I can't understand this for the woods are probably the easiest clubs in the bag for a long, fairly accurate shot. The driver, of course, is used off the tee where you can select your lie and tee up the ball. No other shot in golf offers these advantages.

Wood shots from the fairway also generally present the advantage of a decent lie. Whenever the ball rests in a cupped lie or depression where I am not sure I have a clear path for the clubhead to swing into the ball, I discard the idea of hitting a wood and use an iron.

When thinking of woods, always associate them with distance. Distance is the primary function of a wood shot, while accuracy comes first with the irons. With woods, you have the entire length and width of the fairway as a target area, but iron shots generally are aimed at a much narrower and smaller area—the green.

The driver furnishes the greatest distance of the wood clubs and has the least amount of loft on the club face. This club is used only from the tee except when extra distance is demanded from the fairway and the ball is sitting up pertly.

Next, the brassie or No. 2 wood furnishes your shot slightly less distance than the driver, as it has a little more loft on the club face. The No. 2 wood is used for distances of about 15 to 20 yards less than the driver, or from fairway lies unfavorable for using a driver but where distance is needed.

The No. 3 wood, or spoon, has even more loft on the club face. Consequently, it will get the ball up in the air easier from a close lie. Naturally though, this increased loft of the club face will decrease the distance obtained with this club.

The No. 4 wood represents still another step downward in distance but upward in club face loft. Until a player becomes proficient, it is better to sacrifice a little distance by using the No. 3 wood instead of a brassie, or a No. 4 wood in place of the spoon—especially when the ball's lie is close or cupped. It's mighty important to get that ball up into the air.

Many folks have trouble hitting an accurate long iron shot or experience difficulty in getting such a shot into the air. For these folks, I would recommend using the No. 5 wood which makes getting the ball out of a bad lie downright easy at times.

Although I don't generally carry a No. 5 wood in my bag, it is good for an occasional stroke or two during a round. As a matter of fact, the clubs I carry generally vary according to the course I'm playing and the weather conditions.

For example, if the wind is exceptionally strong, I would not have much opportunity to use a No. 5 wood or perhaps even a No. 4 wood. These clubs would give me too much height which is undesirable on a windy day.

No matter which clubs I use, I always stay within the 14-club limit which is fixed for official play. Even in a practice round, it is wise to observe all the rules and become accustomed to them.

A WOOD FROM THE TEE

The driver is usually the wood club used from the tee because it potentially furnishes more distance than any other club. Occasionally, I use the No. 2 or No. 3 wood from the tee, but in these instances, I am not seeking maximum distance.

The driver from the tee is the easiest of all wood shots because the teeing surface is flat and the ball is teed up. If you muff this shot, the blame must be placed entirely upon you.

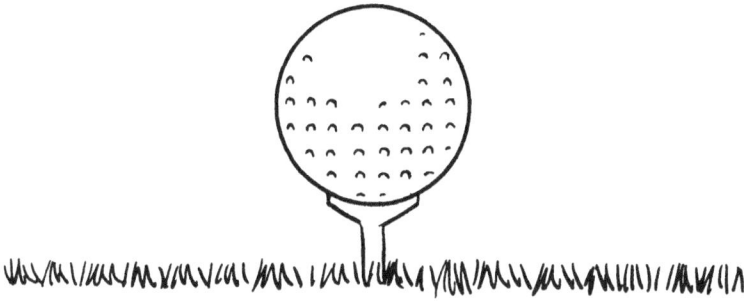

Here is the lie you can have no alibis for. Placed by you, anywhere on the tee you wish, as high as you like. There the ball sits, just waiting for you to smack it!

Balance and relaxation are important in the drive. Sole the club behind the ball, then step into a position that feels comfortable for you. In most cases, this position will be one which places the weight equally upon each foot. The toes should be pointed slightly outward because this is the normal stance for most of us.

If you are standing too close or too far from the ball, your position will feel awkward and off-balance. I use practically a square stance for driving. That is, a line along my toes is almost parallel to the intended line of flight.

The Drive. Study these pictures, adopt any part of my style that seems to fit your own physical make-up, but don't try to copy it. No two people swing alike.

7

Use whichever stance is best adapted to your build and game, but don't employ an *extremely* open or closed stance for the tee shot. Many championship golfers have used the square stance, while others have used the slightly open or closed stance with great success.

The swing should be a relaxed motion. Don't try to "kill" the ball to obtain extra distance. The longest drives from the tee result from free moving, coordinated swings.

Because I have somewhat long arms, I use an upright swing on this tee shot, but this will depend upon the physical characteristics of the individual golfer. A person with short arms and a deep chest will naturally feel freer using a flatter swing.

The chief difference between the upright and the flat swings is that in the latter the body is required to turn more fully than in the former.

Another help in perfecting your swing is to use clubs that are fitted to your build. A short fellow cannot use the same length driver as a tall, lanky golfer. When choosing your equipment, make sure it is right for your own personal needs.

Don't hurry your backswing. Swing the club back at a comfortable pace to a spot where the shaft is about horizontal to the ground. Although some golfers can bring the club back further (including myself), I would not advise it for the average player.

Start the downswing slowly, gradually increasing the tempo until the clubhead reaches its greatest speed just as contact is made with the ball. The clubhead should sweep the ball off the tee just at the bottom of the downswing.

Keep the head down through the swing until after impact with the ball, allowing it, however, to turn with the motion of the body and arms as they carry on to the completion of the stroke.

Remember: balance—relaxation—comfort—are important.

BRASSIE LIES IN THE FAIRWAY

When you find yourself faced with a long shot from the fairway, and the lie of the ball is adequate, the brassie is the club to choose. The loft of the brassie's face will give height to the shot with no lifting effort on your part.

With the driver, my advice was to sweep the ball off the tee or grass at the bottom of the swing. However, in hitting with the brassie, you should hit down, striking the ball on the downswing and taking a bit of turf in front of the ball, unless, of course, the ball is sitting up nicely.

The idea of hitting down and nipping the turf in the follow-through will increase the amount of backspin and thus insure the ball getting well up into the air.

Here is an example of an excellent lie from which to play a brassie shot. Just hit down on the ball—make no effort to scoop it up!

Don't attempt to hit the brassie from a poor lie if you are the least bit unsure of yourself. Whenever in doubt, go to the spoon or the No. 4 wood.

Again, remember the brassie will not get the ball sharply into the air, as will the No. 3 or No. 4 woods. If you don't have enough clearance over an obstacle, forget the brassie.

The important feature in playing the No. 2 wood from a poor lie is in hitting down on the ball. An attempt to sweep the ball or to pick it up, usually will result in a topped or smothered shot.

Swing down on the ball, hitting it first and letting the club face do the lofting for you.

Occasionally you may be faced with a chance to use the driver from the fairway, although there are not too many opportunities to do so.

First of all, you won't play many holes which require two such long pokes (assuming your drive was successful).

Secondly, you must have an excellent lie in order to hit the driver from the fairway, and you don't often find the ball sitting up in such a position. At least I don't.

This shot, when you are faced with it, is played practically the same as the drive from the tee. Sweep the ball from the grass without a conscious attempt to hit up and get the ball into the air.

But because of a doubtful lie or the need for height, you may be hesitant about using the driver from the fairway. By all means then, go to a weaker club which will guarantee getting the ball off the ground and will give you greater confidence in the success of the shot. Use the No. 2 or No. 3 wood.

One position from which you can use a driver with only a fair lie is an uphill position. Because you are almost certain to get the ball into the air easily from this lie, the driver can be employed successfully, thus imparting extra distance to the shot.

SPOON LIES IN THE FAIRWAY

The No. 3 wood shot is less risky than either the driver or the No. 2 wood from the fairway. The club possesses greater loft, can get the ball into the air easier and can be used from lies where the driver and brassie would never be attempted.

Another feature of the No. 3 wood is its ability to loft the ball quickly. If trees, or some other immediate obstacle, make you the least bit doubtful of using a driver or a No. 2 wood, select the spoon, and it will do the job for you.

A lie of this type may well be considered a spoon lie. The lofted face of the spoon can easily get the ball into the air.

The important thing to remember in hitting a spoon shot is to strike the ball first. One method of making sure you hit the ball first is to play the ball back a bit more toward the right foot than the left. In this way, the clubhead strikes the ball a descending blow, helping to get the ball up into the air.

The spoon is a shorter club than either the driver or the brassie, and therefore you will stand a bit closer to the ball when you swing. This will make your swing more upright.

Probably the most important decision you'll make concerning using a spoon from a poor fairway lie is whether you'll use a wood club at all.

In many cases, it is wiser to use an iron because the ball's lie makes it almost impossible to hit a successful wood shot. If the lie is cupped, an iron should be used, for, due to its more narrow sole, the iron can get down at the ball in such a position where a wood cannot.

In all cases, remember the loft on the face of a spoon can help get the ball into the air from some pretty bad lies, so don't sell this club short. If you decide to use the spoon, have confidence that you'll be successful. Don't admit the failure of the shot before you try it. While it is not as easy as a tee shot, you should feel the same confidence.

Remember: hit down on the ball to get it into the air.

You can't be careless in making your decision as to what club to use. Consider the lie, the distance, the layout and the playing conditions.

DON'T USE A WOOD CLUB FOR
THESE FAIRWAY LIES

Although I am a firm admirer of the power of a wood club, there are certain circumstances which force me to advise an iron. Some of these are listed below:

1. When you can reach the green with an iron.

2. When a wood shot will likely reach trouble, such as a hazard.

3. When the fairway is very heavily trapped at about the spot a wood shot would reach. You can "place" an iron better.

4. When the lie is sharply downhill.

5. When some obstruction intervenes and you need an extremely low or extremely high shot to go under or over the obstacle.

6. When your ball has found a very "cuppy" lie.

7. When the ball lies upon badly sun-baked or grass-shy ground.

8. When your ball lies close to the turn of a dog-leg hole, and you can't put a long wood shot either over or around the turn of the fairway.

9. When your swing is restricted and you must use a shorter club.

13

WOODS ARE SELDOM USED IN THE ROUGH

Although I very seldom attempt to use a wood from the rough, the few occasions I do so finds me using either the No. 3 or No. 4 wood.

The lie for such a shot should be fairly good with a clear path for the clubhead to swing into the ball. If the ball is in high grass, I certainly would not advise using a wood. The most important job is to get the ball out of its immediate poor position, and a well-lofted iron is the usual answer. You can't blast a ball through heavy grass with a wood club.

However, you may find yourself faced with a respectable lie in the rough, some distance from the green. In that case, you should select a wood because it will provide the extra distance, where an iron would not.

In some instances, you might stand a bit closer to the ball than for a normal spoon shot, thus using a more upright swing. This is helpful when your swing is restricted or when the path through the grass to the ball is limited.

Use an iron in deep rough—woods don't have the necessary loft.

14

HOW TO CONTROL WOOD SHOTS IN THE WIND

Very seldom will you play golf when there is absolutely no wind at all. In the vast majority of cases, the wind has a definite effect on your shots, and it is up to you to compensate for this effect.

When hitting into a strong wind, the primary object is to keep the ball as low as possible. Otherwise, a ball hit high into a strong wind will have its distance reduced considerably and also is likely to be blown off line.

One method of keeping the ball low with a wood shot is to tee the ball low when driving. At other times, use the lowest numbered wood possible considering the distance needed and the ball's position. A high numbered wood has more loft and gives added height to the ball, making it more susceptible to the wind.

Remember, the wind is working to increase the ball's height and decrease the ball's distance when you are hitting into it.

If the wind is blowing across your shot, I would again advise keeping the ball as low as possible, following the same suggestions listed above. I don't like to depend upon the wind to furnish any added distance or direction; I would much rather supply these things myself.

However, when you face a wind blowing from right to left, you should allow for it in your shot. Gauge the force of the wind and adjust your stance so you are aiming enough to the right of the usual intended line of flight. This aiming to the right will compensate for the effect of the wind upon the ball.

The opposite holds true for a wind blowing from left to right. Aim your shot to the left of your usual line of flight.

In both instances, try to keep the ball as low as possible for this will reduce the effect the wind has on the ball.

Occasionally, expert golfers will use an intentional hook or slice to compensate for such a wind or to clear some obstruction, but I would not recommend these shots for the average golfer. I will discuss these shots later.

Sooner or later, you're bound to be fortunate enough to have the wind with your shot instead of against it. In such an instance, the wind can help you gain extra distance. If you desire this distance, tee the ball higher when using a wood from the tee so the shot can gain plenty of height.

When hitting from the fairway, use the No. 3 or No. 4 wood to impart height to the ball so the wind can add extra yards to your shot.

Judging the speed and direction of the wind is a delicate thing, for the wind is not consistent. It can shift, increase or slow down without warning.

Sometimes, you may not be able to judge the wind at all from where you are playing the shot. I recall that the 17th tee at Medinah Country Club in Chicago is protected on the left by a grove of trees which shield the tee. Yet, the ball must travel from this sheltered position out across a lake to a small green, and there is usually a treacherous wind blowing across the lake making it difficult, if not impossible, to gauge from the tee.

HITTING WOODS FROM HILLY LIES

Uphill Lies

The chief adjustments for an uphill shot with a wood (or an iron, for that matter) are made in the stance.

I like to take my usual stance, and then bend my left knee so my hips and shoulders are near normal when I am addressing the ball. Balance is exceedingly necessary here, however, and I always make sure that bending the knee does help to maintain my balance.

The main point to notice here is that in both the uphill and down-hill lies I keep my stance as normal as possible.

Many golfers have a tendency to hook a shot from an uphill lie. If this is your habit, just aim a bit to the right of the intended line of flight to compensate for the hook.

Because of the unusual stance, your balance may be hampered, and you may tend to hurry this shot. Try some practice swings in this position if you can, and remember to take your time in getting adjusted to the slope.

Usually, it is safe to use a straighter-faced club than the distance calls for when the lie is uphill. Because any shot from this position tends to go high into the air, the extra distance obtained from the straighter-faced club will prove valuable.

Downhill Lies

This downhill shot is more difficult than the uphill shot because of a mental hazard involved. Most golfers feel they will swing into the hill on their downswing before contacting the ball.

I take my usual stance for this shot, and then bend my right knee so the shoulders and hips are nearly level when I am addressing the ball.

I play the ball back toward my right foot, and use a club which is more lofted than is needed for the distance involved. I do this because I am swinging down at the ball, and the club face should be almost vertical when contact is made. The greater loft of the club will compensate for the angle of the hill.

Sidehill Lies—Feet Below the Ball

Perhaps the greatest danger from a sidehill lie with the feet below the ball is the tendency to stand away from the ball and use a baseball swing as though you were reaching for a low outside curve.

In taking your stance, sole the club behind the ball and step into what seems like a comfortable position. You probably will find you need to choke the club slightly, but don't fall into the mistake of the baseball swing.

Here again balance is important. Set your feet and stand erect so you can maintain good balance and prevent this leaning.

Sidehill Lies—Feet Above the Ball

With this shot, too, you will find yourself "leaning" down the hill. Set your feet firmly and far enough apart to avoid this danger. Also increase the normal bending of your knees.

You are likely to want to grip the club on the very end in order to reach the ball. This is all right if it does not feel too awkward for you.

Balance and relaxation are important. You will feel more confident if you perfect this shot in practice. Don't wait until you find yourself faced with a difficult shot before attempting it. Constant practice of these troublesome shots will make them seem ordinary when facing them in a competitive round.

SOMETIMES YOU *WANT* TO SLICE OR HOOK

How to Slice

Although most golfers are more concerned with preventing slices than deliberately cultivating them, there are occasions when an intentional slice is helpful. I would advise such a shot only for the more advanced golfer, however.

I obtain this slice, or fade to the right, by opening my stance slightly and playing the ball farther up toward my left foot. The clubhead then will strike the ball in a motion of cutting across from the outside in, making the ball curve to the right.

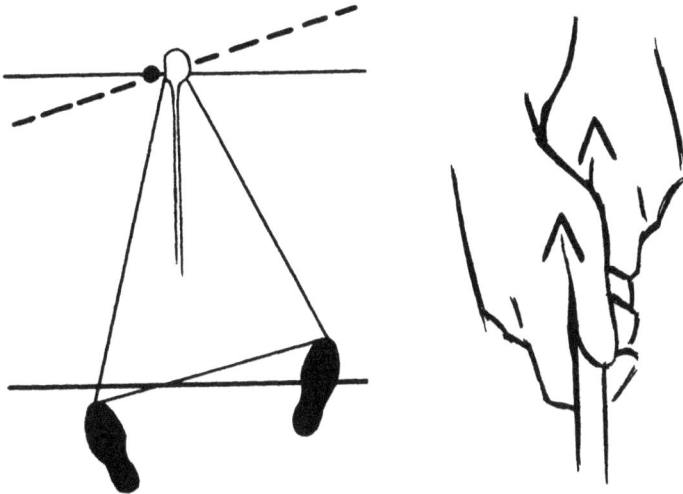

Open the stance and shift the grip to the left on the shaft.

Another aid to slicing is in changing the grip slightly. I allow my thumbs to rest more on top of the grip. This will place my hands in such a position that the V's formed by the thumb and forefinger of each hand point more toward my chin than toward the right shoulder, which is the normal direction.

19

How to Hook

In using a deliberate hook, I again warn the beginning golfer to stay away from such a shot. Only after you have mastered the basic shots of golf would I advise you to consider these useful but dangerous shots.

The intentional hook is obtained by closing the stance and striking the ball by bringing the club face from the "inside-out."

Another danger with the intentional hook and slice is in practicing the very faults which you are striving to eliminate from your game. Don't let them slip into a regular part of your swing.

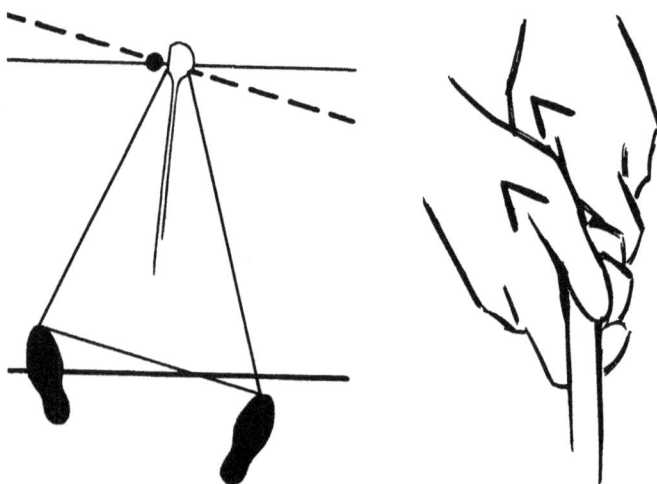

Close the stance and shift the grip to the right on the shaft.

The grip, for example, is changed slightly for the intentional hook. The hands will grip the club more toward the right side of the shaft, and the V's will point toward the right upper arm— below the right shoulder. This will automatically bring about a face-closing on the club, without which hooking is impossible.

THE GENERAL USE OF THE IRONS

As I stated earlier, accuracy is the prime objective of the iron clubs. You are not only concerned with hitting a crisp shot, but you are aiming at a green that is usually no more than 20 yards wide and your shot should not fall short, go beyond or to either side of this target.

Naturally, with such a limited target area, you must be very accurate. However, the golf club manufacturers have helped by designing the irons with accuracy in mind. The shafts are shorter for irons than for woods, giving you better control of the club. This shorter shaft places the golfer closer to the ball and necessitates a more upright swing.

The irons range from the No. 2 iron through the No. 9. They can be easily classified into three categories—the long irons are the Nos. 2 and 3; the medium irons are the Nos. 4, 5 and 6; while the No. 7, 8 and 9 are called the short irons.

The lower the number of the iron, the less loft on the club face and the greater the distance to be gained from the shot. Usually, every iron shot is intended to reach the green. If you don't believe an iron shot will reach the green, you should use a wood.

The long irons are used when distance is called for, plus accuracy, or when distance alone is needed but the lie makes using a wood risky. The medium irons—particularly the No. 5 iron—are extremely versatile and sometimes serve the purposes of both long and short irons. The short irons are generally used for close approach shots and also for the trouble shots—from sand, rough or high grass.

I generally carry about 10 irons in my bag, with the number and selection varying. I would suggest the No. 2 through the No. 9 iron plus a sand wedge and putter for the average golfer. At times I carry a driving iron where the course demands accuracy from the tee above every other requirement.

There has never been a putter made that sinks them all, but I have enjoyed my greatest success in recent years using a modified center-shafter putter.

Choose your clubs carefully; they play a big part in your scoring ability.

Here is illustrated the decisive moment of iron play. The club, instead of "sweeping" the ball away at the low point of the swing, hits DOWN ONTO the ball in a crisp, decisive manner. The club then continues its arc, swinging into the turf and taking the divot AFTER the ball has been struck.

SOME TEE SHOTS REQUIRE
AN IRON

On short holes an iron is used, rather than a wood, in playing from the tee. Many players do not use a tee for this shot, preferring to hit the ball from the surface of the ground. I would recommend this when you are hitting into a heavy wind, and you want to keep the shot as low as possible. Since you are using an iron, you should have no difficulty in getting the ball up into the air. In hitting the ball from atop a tee, you are likely to give too much height to the shot, thereby sacrificing some of the needed distance.

However, if you desire to use a tee (as many fine players do), it is not necessary to tee the ball high as the iron can get the ball up easily.

The swing for this shot is much the same as for driving with a wood, except for the closer stance to the ball and more upright swing. The ball should be swept off the tee or turf where it is sitting.

Start your backswing slowly with no conscious attempt to rush into the stroke. Don't try to shorten the length of the backswing. It is natural in swinging an iron to take a shorter backswing. Don't force any part of the iron shot. Remember you are aiming for the green, and any unnatural movement certainly will ruin your accuracy.

On the next two pages are sketches of the way I use a long iron club. You may find some ideas that you can fit to your own play.

25

THE USE OF THE LONG IRONS

Long irons are considered the most difficult of the iron clubs by many golfers, but I don't agree. Most of the trouble befalling a golfer using a long iron is a result of his trying to force extra distance from the club.

Whenever you are the least bit doubtful of achieving the distance required with the club you have selected, move back a notch to the next most powerful club. This advice also applies when you are playing into a wind, and your normal distance with a club is reduced.

For a long iron shot from a good lie, I like to play the ball up a bit toward the left foot so the club contacts the ball just as the sole of the clubhead is at the bottom of its arc.

When the ball rests in a cupped lie and distance is still required, you should choose the long iron which has the greatest chance of getting the ball out of its position and into the air. This is left to your own judgment, but don't overestimate your ability with the No. 2 iron. It is better to use a No. 3 iron and fall 10 yards short of the green than to try the No. 2 iron and top or only half-hit the ball.

The swing in such a case should be altered slightly. Try to strike the ball on the downswing instead of taking it flush with the surface. This will aid in getting the ball into the air. To aid in striking the ball on the downswing, play the ball farther back toward the right foot than would be the case if the lie were good.

The grip for all long iron shots should be definitely firm. Because you are taking the ball and turf, the tendency for the club to twist in the hands is greater than with a wood. Any tendency toward looseness in the grip will allow the club to get out of control.

THE USE OF THE MEDIUM IRONS

As you move into the medium irons from the long irons, there are several changes necessary.

First, the ball is played back toward the center of the two feet so it is struck a descending blow by the club face. The greater loft on the club face lifts the ball with no lifting motion required in the swing.

Second, the backswing is shortened. As the distance needed in the shot becomes shorter, so the swing of the club becomes less full. This shorter backswing should come naturally, however, if your stance is correct for the club you're using.

Third, the stance should be opened more with each higher-numbered club. This open stance brings the right side of the body around and prevents an excessive backswing.

Familiarize yourself with the distance you can obtain from each of the medium irons so you'll have no difficulty in choosing the proper club for each shot. Practice is the only sure method I have ever found for gaining this important knowledge.

My favorite club among the medium irons is the No. 5 iron, and I give it most of my medium iron play. I use it from good lies and poor lies alike and find it a most versatile club. Sometimes I use it for short chip shots to the green.

In hitting this iron from a poor lie, apply the principle of hitting down on the ball and striking it first. Without this fundamental, the shot is doomed to failure regardless of how well you execute the other parts of the stroke.

Since the medium irons are so named, you can easily remember that the ball generally is played about midway between the two feet for shots with these clubs. This will vary, to use an old Army phrase, "according to the situation and the terrain."

27

THE PLAY OF THE SHORT IRONS

The short irons generally are called the pitching irons because that is their chief function. However, they also are used, as occasions arise, from sand traps, rough and high grass.

In using these clubs—the No. 7, 8 and 9 irons—the stance is closer to the ball and more open. As the distance for the ball to travel is reduced, the backswing is shortened proportionately. This places the major responsibility for this shot on the hands and arms, and body action becomes a more passive than active means of power.

At the top of the backswing, the club is in an upright position, illustrating the shortness of the swing with these clubs. If you feel you are reaching or stretching in swinging down on the ball, you are probably standing too far from the ball. The follow-through with the pitching irons is regulated by the force generated from the back swing. However, the club face must always follow-through the ball.

If you swing down on the ball and strike it first before taking up turf, your hands are certain to be slightly ahead of the ball at the moment of contact. This helps guide the shot and should be desired in practicing the short iron stroke.

In addition to their reputation as pitching irons, the short irons are also called trouble irons. The reason for this name will become apparent to you after you've used them from lies and situations which are extremely disagreeable, to say the least.

Whenever the ball is lying in high grass and heavy rough, one of these well-lofted irons is the club to lift it out of there. You have practically to blast your way through heavy grass.

If an immediate obstacle must be cleared, once more you must use the pitching iron to gain the necessary elevation for the ball.

An expert with the short irons can atone for many mistakes with his longer clubs by recovering from bad lies and spanking a pitch shot high into the air and dropping the ball on the green.

It is most important to strike the ball first without losing any momentum by hitting the turf or any other obstacle first. This, plus the club face loft, will lift the ball out of its troublesome lie.

Although many players like to shorten up and "choke" the grip of the club for such a short iron shot, I don't usually do that. I like to use my normal grip up near the top of the leather and take as full a swing as the situation warrants.

The swing for the irons, especially the short irons, is marked by a closer-to-the-ball stance, and a relatively short backswing. It is also quite apparent that there is much less body turn than when the longer clubs are used.

MANY IRON SHOTS MUST BE PLAYED FROM HILLY LIES

Downhill Lies

In taking your stance for a downhill lie with an iron, the right knee should be bent in a bit toward the ball. This aids your balance and brings your stance to a more level plane.

The body should lean slightly to the right further to aid in balancing yourself for the shot. Play the ball back toward the right foot, regardless of what numbered iron you use.

The natural tendency for most golfers is to slice this downhill shot. I correct this by using a well-lofted club and closing the club face. This also seems to give me some added power in striking the ball.

Uphill Lies

For playing some lies there is no such thing as "form." The position that enables you to maintain your balance and swing through the ball is the correct one.

An uphill iron shot should be played very similarly to an uphill wood shot. Bend the left knee slightly to bring the hips and shoulders in a more level line. In bending the left knee and taking your position for this shot, be certain you have a good balance before addressing the ball. Perhaps you might lean a bit forward to prevent falling backwards away from the shot. The ball should be played a bit forward toward the left foot, and you should use a lower-numbered club than you would normally choose for the distance. Since your swing will not be as full and some distance will be lost due to excess altitude, a more powerful club will compensate for these factors.

Sidehill Lies—Feet Below the Ball

In adjusting your stance for a sidehill iron shot with the ball above the feet, your weight must be concentrated on the balls of your feet and your toes. Should you swing with the weight back on the heels, you will fall away from the shot and either top the ball or miss it entirely.

I prefer to play the ball midway between the two feet and choke up a bit on the club. There is a tendency to hook this shot, but facing slightly to the right of your objective will compensate for this danger.

Sidehill Lies—Feet Above Ball

The stance on this occasion places the weight back on the heels to prevent pitching forward into the shot. The club should be gripped on the end, and the ball played midway between the two feet.

The tendency here is to slice, but this can be allowed for by merely aiming slightly to the left of your objective.

In any troublesome shot of this type, balance is exceedingly important. It is more than half the battle.

PLAYING IRON SHOTS ON
WINDY DAYS

Hitting With the Wind

Hitting with the wind will affect iron shots more than wood shots due to the increased height obtained from irons.

A suitable allowance should be made for the extra distance which the wind will add to your iron shot. Otherwise, you will find yourself learning how to pitch out from the woods or other trouble beyond the green. This is merely a matter of judgment on your part.

Consider the club you normally would use for such a distance and then select at least one number higher to compensate for the added length the wind will furnish your shot.

Hitting Against the Wind

In hitting an iron shot into the wind, keep in mind the same things I mentioned concerning the wood clubs.

Use the lowest numbered iron possible which the ball's position will permit. The long irons are particularly well-adapted for hitting into a wind as they will give long distance without lifting the ball too high.

Remember, too, the wind will diminish your distance no matter how expertly you hit the shot. To compensate for this loss, you should study the force of the wind and choose a club at least one number stronger than your usual choice for the same distance.

How Cross Winds Affect Iron Shots

Wind blowing across the intended line of flight of your ball can play havoc with an otherwise perfect shot. Because the irons lift a ball more than woods, the wind has more effect upon such shots.

Iron shots being intended primarily for accuracy, the slightest deviation from their regular path can prove fatal—sending the ball into a trap or heavy rough surrounding the green.

You must estimate how much the wind will affect your shot and compensate for this by aiming slightly into the wind and allowing the wind to blow the ball back into the regular line.

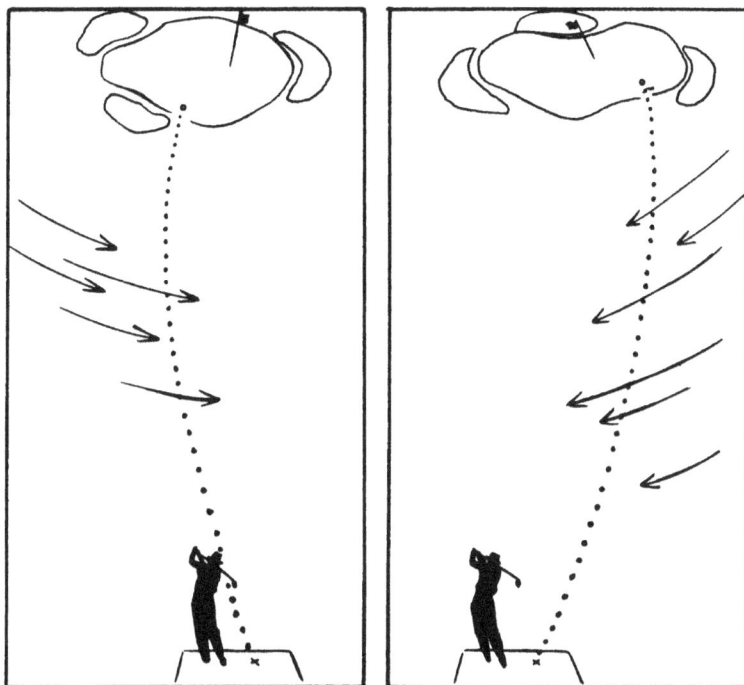

Play your shot a little bit into a strong wind blowing across the line of flight—to the right of your objective when the wind is from right to left, to the left of your target when it blows from left to right.

AN IRON WILL GET THE BALL
OUT OF TROUBLE

When Playing From Light Rough

When playing from the light rough for either long or short distance, your problem is not too great. You almost can play the shot as though it were in the fairway.

If distance is required, stand back and take a full swing. For a short pitch shot, stand closer and use a more upright swing.

Hit the ball first, before taking turf, in either instance. Don't let the grass slow your clubhead before contact. If you keep the club face slightly open, it will help get the ball into the air.

When you have a lie in the rough something like this your choice of an iron should depend upon distance wanted or type of shot desired; practically any iron can be played successfully here.

When Playing From Heavy Rough

The first objective facing a golfer in high, heavy grass is getting the ball out of that position. Obtaining distance is secondary.

I recommend a well-lofted club—a No. 8 or No. 9 iron or perhaps a sand wedge—for getting the necessary height to move the ball out of the immediate high grass, even though it will not contribute much distance. If you employ a slightly less-lofted club, open the club face so the necessary loft is given to the ball immediately.

Use an upright swing from a stance close to the ball and strike the ball on the downswing. Make sure with your upright swing that the heavy grass does not rob the club of its momentum before it contacts the ball.

When you have put yourself in rough of this nature, your concern is to GET OUT. You'll have to figure that it cost you a stroke when you put the ball in; try get out onto the nearest piece of fairway without throwing away additional shots.

HOW TO GET EXTRA HEIGHT
ON A BALL

Immediate height is needed when you are shooting over an obstacle, and the surest method of obtaining this is to use a well-lofted club and hit down on the ball. The combination of these two factors will produce maximum height.

The common fault in this shot is trying to scoop the ball with the clubhead instead of hitting down on the ball and letting the loft of the club face do the work. The usual result finds the club striking behind the ball and taking up turf before striking the ball. This only results in loss of power in the shot.

This fault can be avoided by playing the ball up close to the left foot, from where the clubhead will impart an extra "lift" to it.

HOW TO KEEP A BALL LOW
IN THE AIR

If you find yourself with a shot that must be played low to avoid obstacles such as tree branches, you should forget about any very great distance with the stroke. Clearing the ball under the hanging obstacle calls for a low shot which may not carry far.

Choose an iron without too much loft—a No. 3 or No. 4 iron may do—and play the ball back toward the right foot. Close club face slightly and play ball a little farther from your body; this will tend to give you a somewhat flatter swing.

Take a full swing and carry your motion through as on any other iron shot. Don't halt after striking the ball in the mistaken belief that this chopping motion will keep the ball low. This merely serves to cut down your power and distance still more.

OCCASIONALLY YOU WOULD LIKE TO PUT A CURVE ON AN IRON SHOT

Before telling you how to cultivate an intentional slice or hook with an iron, I want to warn you again that these shots are only for the expert golfer. Otherwise, you are liable to find yourself unconsciously slipping into some bad habits.

A slice can be produced by opening the stance and changing the grip as I mentioned before in discussing a similar shot with the woods. Allow the thumbs to rest more on top of the shaft so the V's are pointing toward the chin. These changes will cause the clubhead, with the face open, to strike the ball as it is moving from the outside in, and produce a slice.

The opposite motions will give you an intentional hook. Close the stance and grip the club more toward the right side of the grip, pointing the V's below the right shoulder. The motion of the clubhead, the face closed, is now from the inside out, as it comes to the ball.

In either case the side spin which is given to the ball from the motion of the clubhead will produce the slice or the hook—whichever is desired.

There are quite a few opportunities to use a CONTROLLED hook or slice. Properly executed, they'll save you a stroke or two every so often. But unless you have the form for the straight shots well drilled into your muscles, there is real danger in practicing these fancy shots. There is no more unhappy golfer than the chronic hooker or slicer!

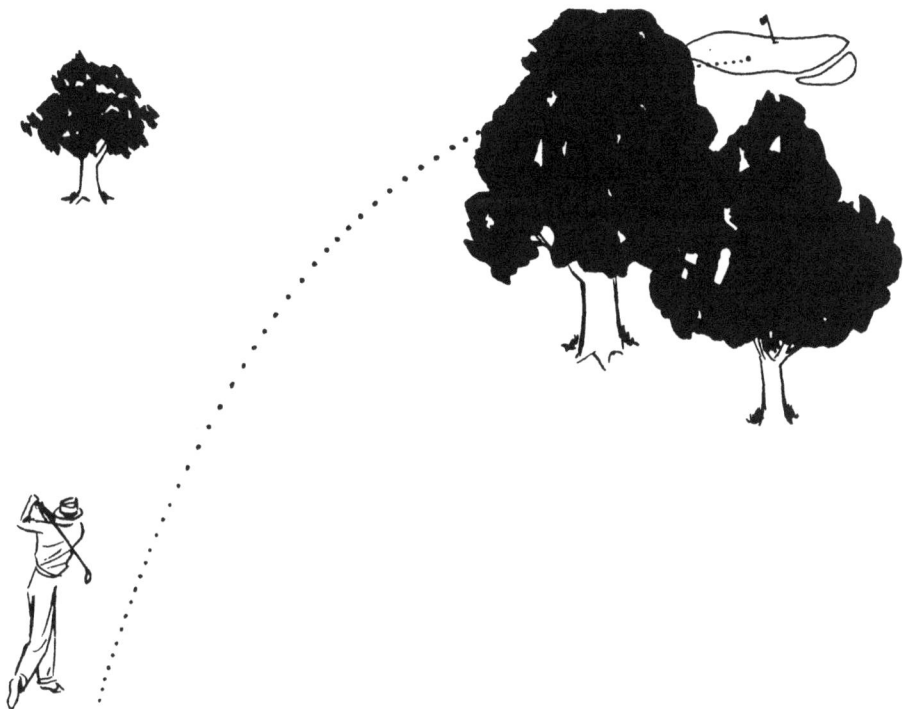

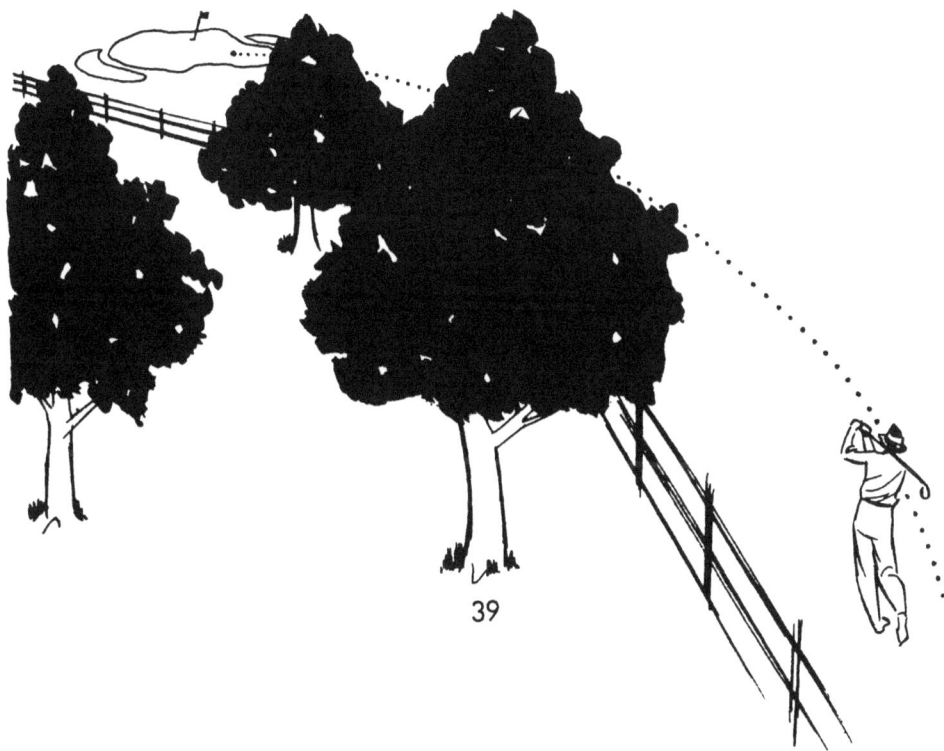

39

THE PITCH SHOT

The pitch shot is a valuable stroke in that it enables the golfer to clear traps, trees and other hazards between the ball and the green.

Because the shot is a high one, I use a pitching niblick, but a No. 8 or No. 9 iron can serve as well. The pitch can be played from a position just off the green up to 120 yards or so away. There is a minimum of roll in the pitch shot, and the ball is aimed directly for the pin.

The backswing and follow-through on this shot are controlled by the length of the shot. For short pitches, the backswing is very short; how short, is a relative matter for each individual to discover for himself. The hands and arms do most of the work in these pitch shots, and there is a minimum of body movement.

I don't consciously open or close the club face for this shot. I keep it square to the intended line of flight. Don't baby the shot, fearing it will go too far. Be firm in your stroke and follow-through completely.

The pitch shot is played right to the hole—don't be short, because you are playing it NOT to run. This shot isn't indicated if the greens are dry and hard, because in that case the backspin can't get a "bite."

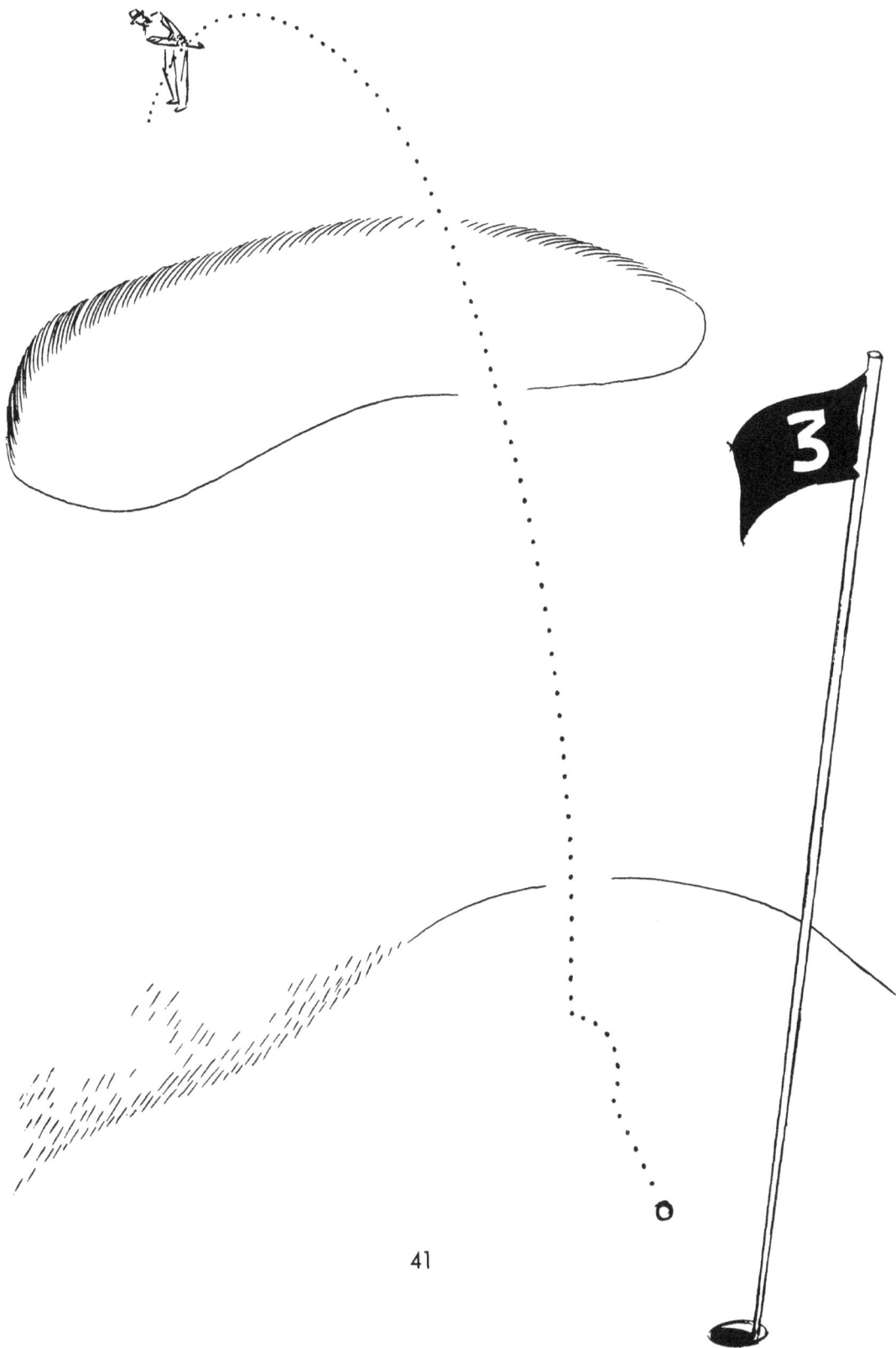

PITCH AND RUN SHOT

The pitch and run shot is very similar to the run-up approach except it is used from longer distances and the path from the ball to the green need not be open. The ball is played deliberately short of the pin, allowing for the ball to roll on toward the hole after it lands.

Often, the pitch and run is used to clear a trap or bunker close to the green.

Since this shot necessarily must be played high, a well-lofted club is used, and the ball is played well back toward the right foot. Any of the short irons can be used—the Nos. 7, 8 or 9 iron —for this shot, depending upon the distance and your own personal choice.

Although this shot is not used too often by most tournament golfers, occasions will arise where it meets the situation's requirements perfectly, such as when the green is very fast, and holding a normal pitch shot is dangerous. This shot can be played from as far away as 100 or 120 yards.

By playing the blade of your club in a somewhat shut or closed position, your ball will roll somewhat after falling on the green in front of the cup.

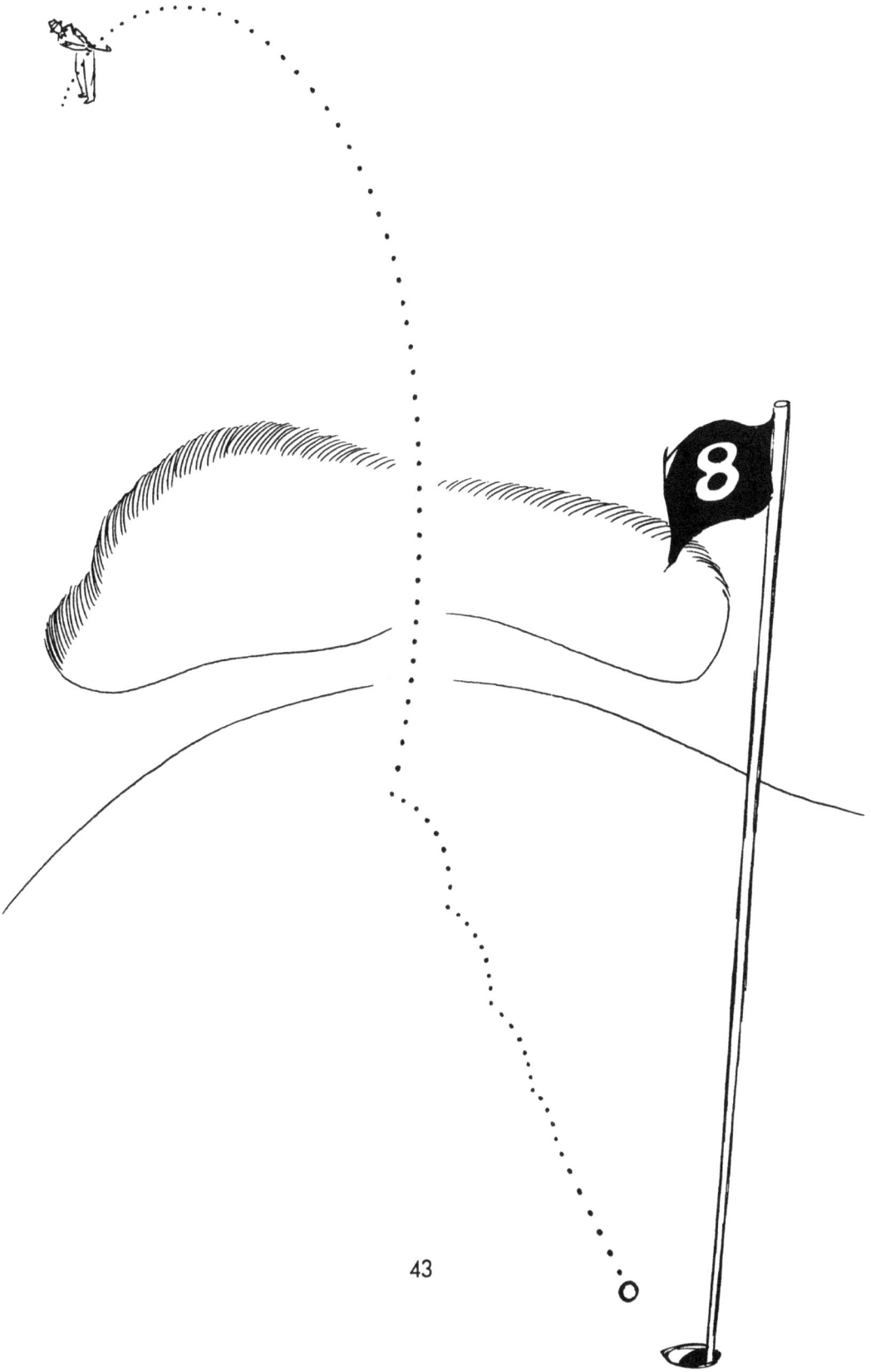

43

THE CHIP SHOT

The chip shot is similar to the pitch and run approach, except it generally is executed with a comparatively straight-faced club such as the No. 5 iron. Naturally, there is not as much height to this shot as to the pitch or pitch and run.

The secret is in knowing where to drop the shot so it will roll up close to the hole. It is strictly a matter of judgment. The chip is played from distances just off the green on up to 100 yards.

I use a comfortable, upright stance for this shot with the ball played just back of the left heel toward center. The amount of power in the shot—and the length of the backswing and follow-through—is determined by the distance the shot must travel.

Remember, however, to be decisive. Don't restrict the follow-through by stopping or slowing down after hitting the ball.

A fine method of practice for the chip shot—and all irons—is to start hitting from just off the green, constantly moving back away from the hole. In this way you'll learn the maximum distance you can obtain with your various clubs and also which clubs you can use for the various shots.

Here is a shot to which you should devote some real practice. You'll probably use it often. It is quite important to hit down on the ball—for unless you "pinch" it that way it may run on and on after it lands on the green.

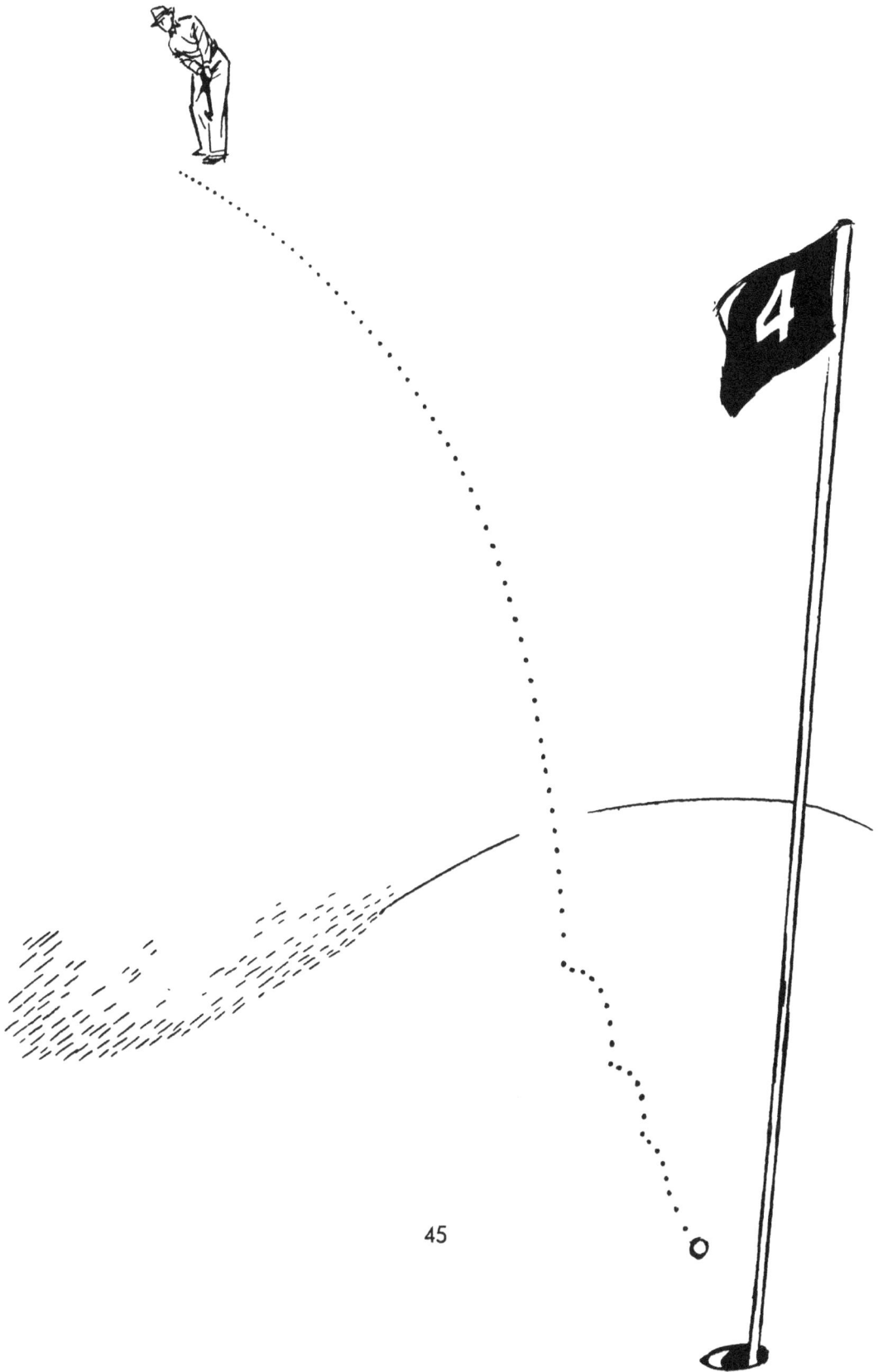

THE CUT SHOT

Playing from the rough or from a sand trap, the cut shot will help you hold the green once the ball hits it. The shot is executed from an open stance with an open club face. This brings the club face across from the outside in and imparts a spin to the ball which takes effect and halts the ball shortly after it lands.

This shot is played forward with the ball almost opposite the left heel and calls for plenty of wrist action.

When played from a sand trap, this shot should have a thin cushion of sand between the ball and the clubhead when contact is made. I would use a sand iron or a No. 9 iron for the shot. If the ball is buried in a sand trap, I would not recommend the cut shot. The ordinary explosion shot will do the job and be less risky.

If, however, you enjoy an excellent lie in a trap, the cut shot can be used to good advantage.

Another method of opening the club face for this shot is in moving your grip slightly to the left so the V's point at the chin instead of the right shoulder.

Open the stance and open the club face. Hit from the "outside in." Do this correctly and your ball will stop on a dime when it lands.

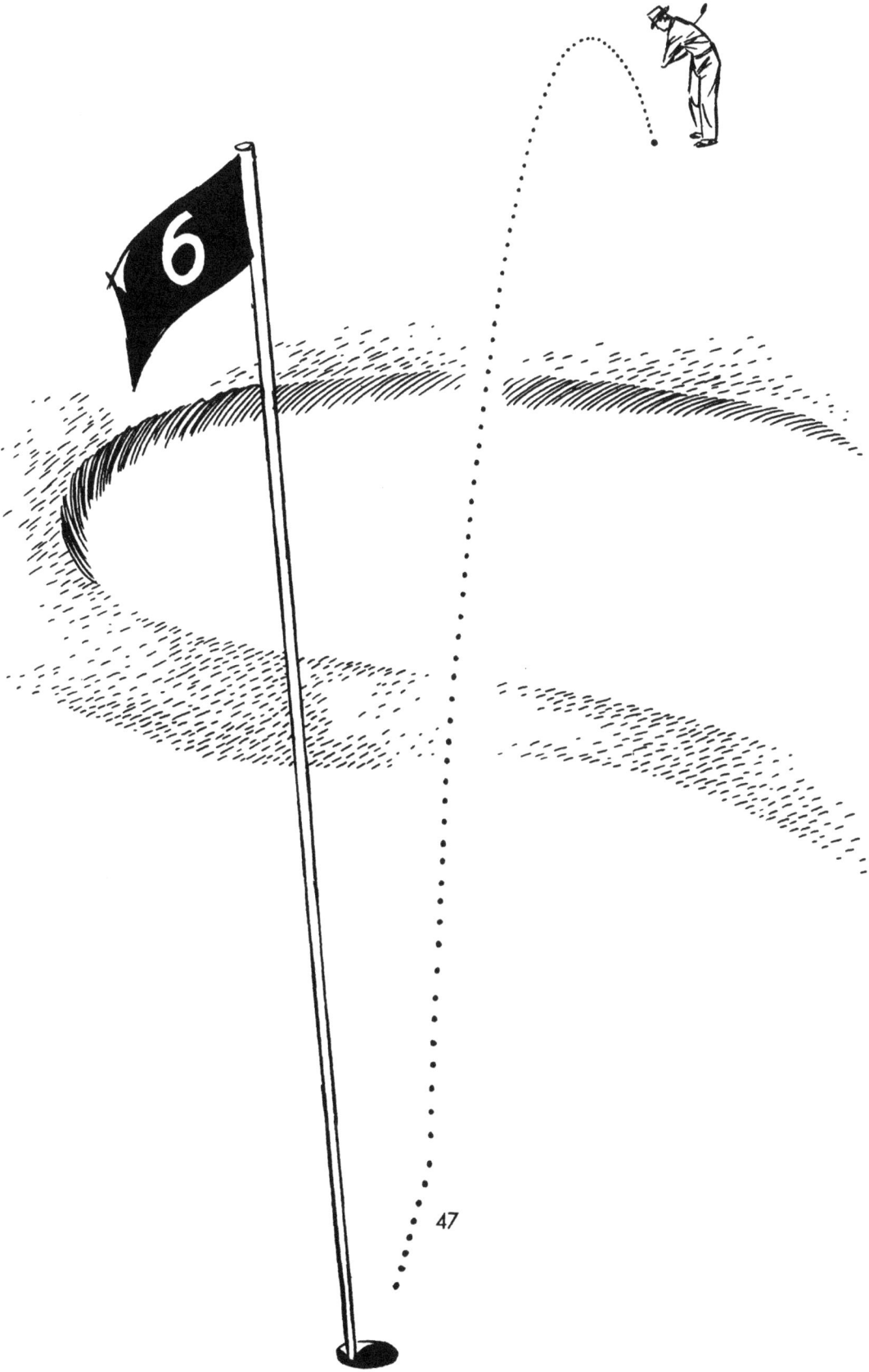

47

THE RUN-UP APPROACH

The run-up approach is used for short distance shots to the green when the path between the ball and the green is open and free of traps or bunkers. The ball is played so it will fall short of the green, then roll on toward the hole.

Many golfers prefer this type of shot to the usual pitch shot which lands on the green. This run-up approach is particularly useful when the green is hard and dry and holding a pitch shot becomes a hazardous risk.

The ball is played back toward the right foot, and the stroke is a firm, downward motion. There is only a minimum of body motion in the shot, the wrist and forearms doing the work. The fullness of the swing will depend upon the distance of the ball from the green.

I would not recommend using this shot from more than 20 or 30 yards away from the green. Since there is little height to the shot, the ball bounces over the grass and rolls onto the green. Any irregularities in the grass leading to the green will throw the ball off its course if the ball strikes them.

For this shot the club comes into the ball from the "inside out" because you don't want to cut down on the run of the ball. This is a popular shot, but you should be aware of the chance you always take that the ball will hit some uneven spot on the fairway and be thrown off course, or stopped short of your objective.

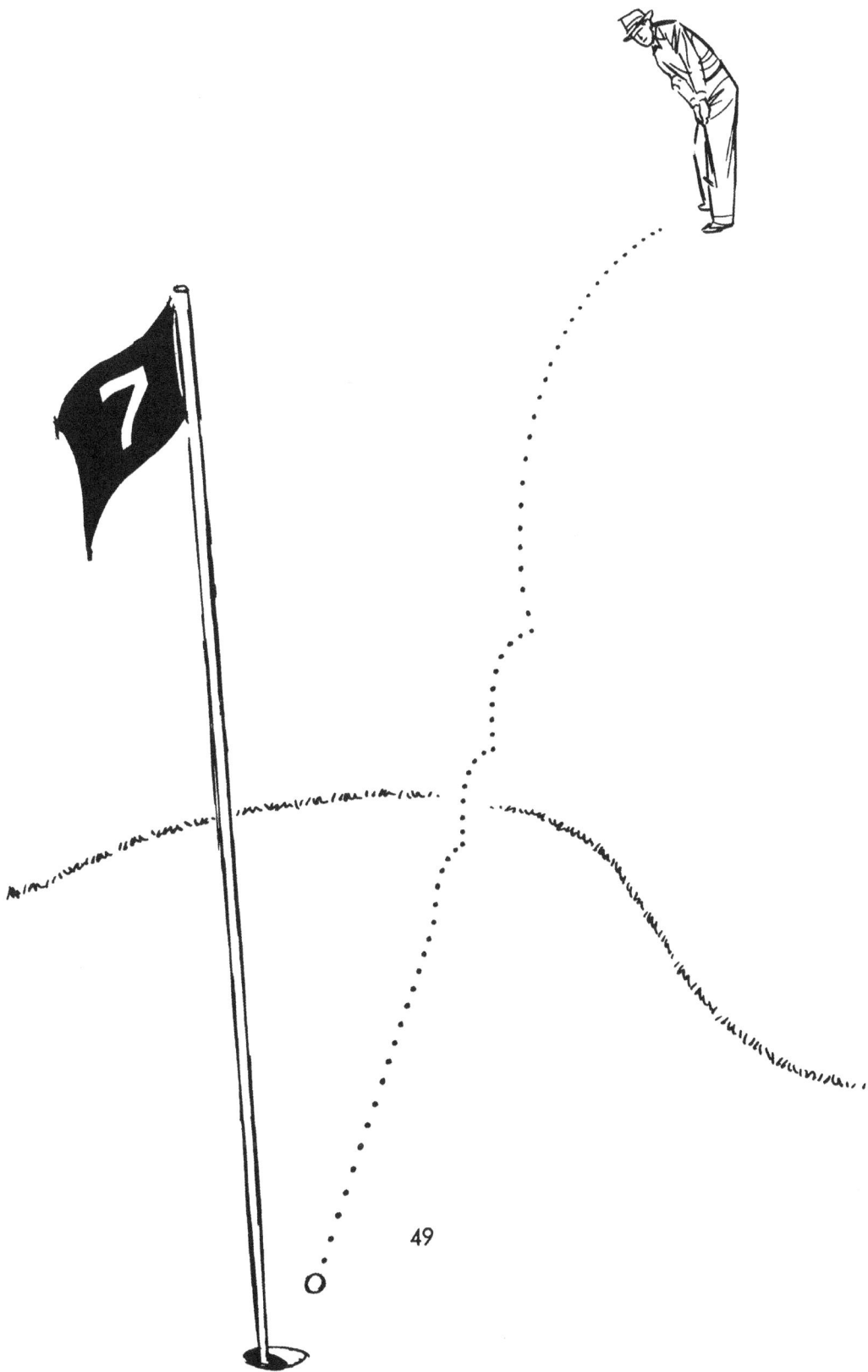

49

APPROACHING FROM SHORT GRASS JUST OFF THE GREEN

The golfer usually has the option of using a chip shot or a glorified putt when the ball is lying in short grass just off the green.

The chip, of course, is made with a No. 5 or similar iron and very little height is given the shot. The object is merely to lift the ball over the short grass and onto the smoother grass of the green, letting the ball roll on to the hole.

When the grass is loose or tending to be sandy, and the ball is very close to the green, you may prefer to use a putter. In this case, stroke the ball as you would a long putt of equal length with no attempt to lift the ball.

During the 1949 National Open at Chicago's Medinah Country Club, I was faced with just such a shot on the tricky 17th hole.

My first shot on this par 3 hole left me on the short grass about 18 inches from the green itself. After studying the situation carefully (at this point I needed pars on the final two holes to tie Cary Middlecoff for the championship), I decided to putt.

I struck the ball firmly, but it leaped into the air over the short grass, onto the green and rolled several feet beyond the hole.

I took two more putts, bogied the hole and had to settle for a second place tie in the Open.

Since then, many people have berated me for using a putter from the short grass, but I still believe it was the right club. My mistake was in not studying the lie of the ball carefully enough. Had I looked a bit closer, I would have noticed the ball was lying in a slight depression. Thus, when I made contact with it, the ball jumped up and over the short grass.

If the ball had *rolled* over this grass on the fringe, I believe it would have slowed down considerably and stopped close to the pin.

And, while blowing the shot was my own fault, I still maintain I chose the right club and the right shot.

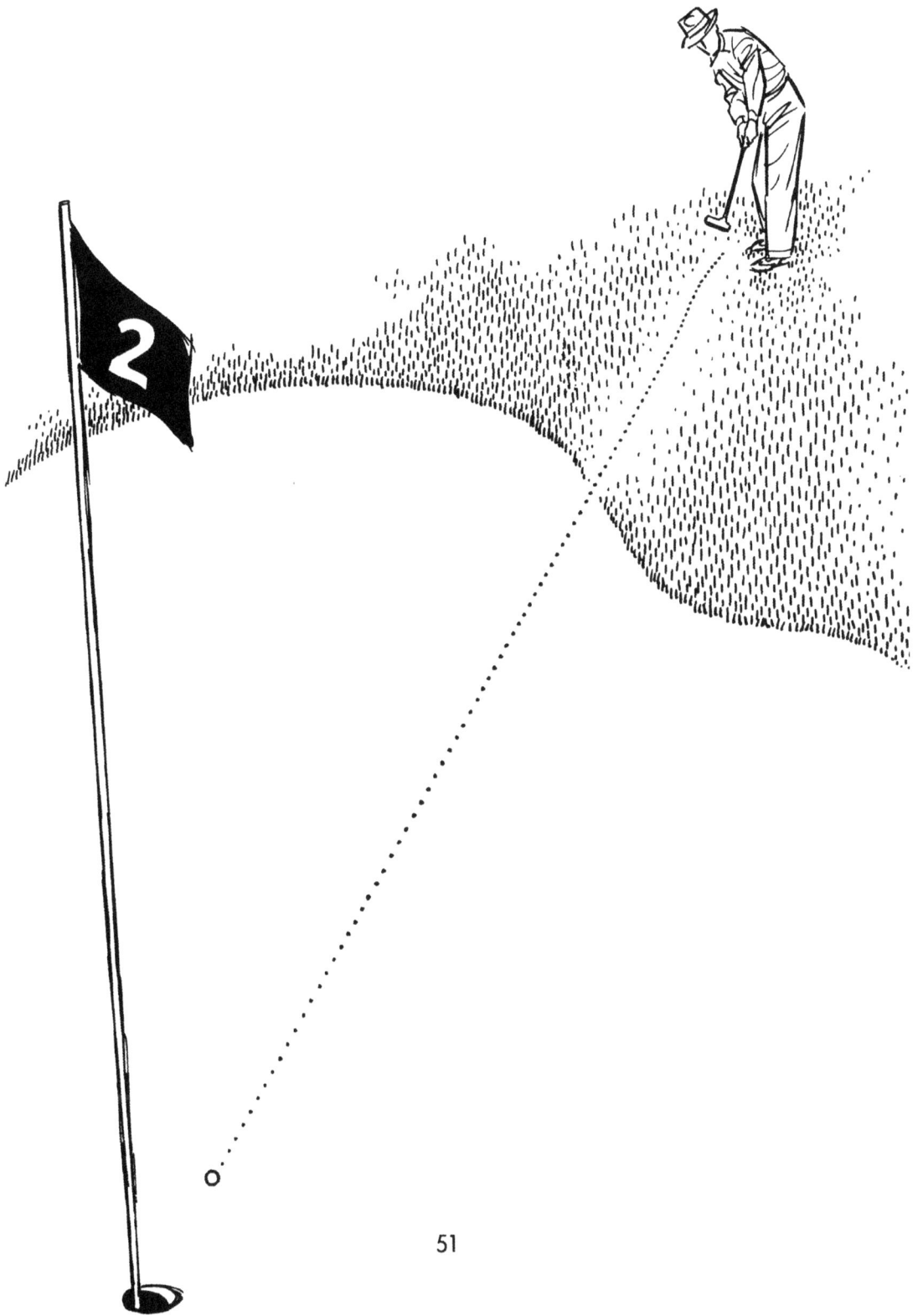

WHAT'S THE DIFFERENCE BETWEEN A FULL-IRON AND A HALF-IRON SHOT?

The chief difference between a full-iron shot and a half-iron shot is in the length and amount of power in the swing.

I would advise using a club which will reach your objective (the green) without undue strain upon the golfer. For example, if I were faced with a shot which would require a full No. 7 iron at its very maximum distance, I would be inclined to use a No. 6 iron and avoid the strain of forcing the No. 7 iron for distance.

In using the No. 6 iron, I obtain the distance a bit more easily than with the No. 7, and since I am not forcing the shot, I have better control of it.

THE PUNCH SHOT

The punch or push shot derives its name from the technique developed by seaside players to contend with strong head winds. In this shot, the ball's flight is kept quite low. Its execution calls for an extra short grip of the club, the keeping of most of the weight over the left foot throughout the swing, and the hitting down on the ball more pronouncedly than is the case with regular iron shots.

The practical effect of the foregoing is to reduce the normal loft of the club used. Thus, by striking nearer the equator of the ball, it (the ball) is caused to take a much lower flight than would normally result.

In the playing of the shot to best results, take a limited backswing. With both arms firmly extended, the hands are used for the vigorous acceleration of the club in hitting the downward blow to the ball.

SOME LIES REALLY ARE
UNPLAYABLE

The rule for unplayable lies states "the player is the sole judge as to when his ball is unplayable. It may be declared unplayable at any place on the course."

The rule further states if a ball "be deemed by the player to be unplayable, the player shall play his next stroke as nearly as possible at the spot from which the ball which is unplayable was played, adding a penalty stroke to the score for the hole."

I would not be too quick to call a shot unplayable. There are times when careful study of a ball's position will suggest a method of hitting the ball from an "unplayable" lie. I have even swung left-handed at a ball when I couldn't swing from my normal position.

At times, however, I feel that calling the ball unplayable and taking the penalty stroke is a wise move rather than risk several shots in a futile attempt to dislodge the ball from its resting place. Back in the 1930's some unfortunate golfer took a 16 on one hole in the National Open because he kept trying to play his ball instead of calling it unplayable.

ON SOME SHOTS YOU CANNOT
GET A FULL SWING AT THE BALL

In a shot made when the swing is restricted, the work must necessarily be done by the hands, wrists and forearms. Since the backswing cannot be a natural, full motion, there is a minimum of body movement and shoulder power in the downswing.

Your choice of a club will depend upon the distance required for the shot and the lie of the ball. Although I do not like to "choke" the club, preferring to grip the club near the top of the leather, it is sometimes necessary to do this when the swing is restricted, and you haven't much room.

Because you are losing power by being unable to take a full swing, you are likely to attempt to make up for this by forcing your hands and wrists to supply extra power. *This is a mistake!*

Settle for a shot of medium power which gets you out into the fairway, rather than trying to "kill" the ball. If the ball must be kept low, close the face of the club.

Before attempting this shot, practice several backswings from the restricted position so you know how full a swing you can negotiate. Remember, however, *take it easy!*

PLAYING TO A HIGHER
OR A LOWER LEVEL

A pitch shot is needed when the ball is lying below an elevated green and you must reach the green. It is desirable to impart some cut or backspin to the ball so it will stop shortly after it strikes the green. Balls hit from a lower to a higher level normally have a tendency to run after striking the green.

I use a pitching niblick for this shot, but a No. 8 or No. 9 iron will suffice. The stance is narrow and slightly open with the head almost directly over the ball. The stroke is executed by the hands and arms with little body motion.

Stopping the shot when it hits the green is important. Otherwise, the ball will roll off the elevated green, and you'll find yourself pitching to an elevated green all over again.

When pitching a shot to a green on a lower level, you can count on the ball's stopping very shortly after it strikes the surface, and you should aim the shot to hit fairly close to the pin. The amount of roll will depend on the angle at which the ball falls to the green.

BACKSPIN WITH THE IRONS

Hitting a shot with backspin is no problem—not even for the beginning golfer. In fact, it is almost unavoidable as every shot carries backspin.

The effort to attain extra backspin is purely a matter of applying an overdose of it to the ball, thereby causing the ball to stop almost as soon as it hits the green.

The extra "reverse English" is attained first by playing the ball forward almost off the left foot. The stance should be open and very narrow. Then, strike the ball sharply and keep the clubhead moving "through" the ball.

TWO FAULTS: UNDER-CLUBBING AND OVER-CLUBBING

The problem of over-clubbing and under-clubbing is one which is entirely mental. The over-clubber will use a club that provides more distance than is needed, while the under-clubber will fall short of the green through using a weaker club than the situation demands.

The general tendency among golfers is to under-club, probably due to a fear of hitting beyond the green, and also to over-rating their ability.

When you're not sure of which club to use, consider the green's surroundings in making your choice. If the green is heavily trapped to the front and comparatively open to the rear, use the stronger iron. You'll be in less trouble here if you over-club.

With the situation reversed and woods or rough are behind the green with the front open, go to the weaker club.

PLAYING A BALL OUT OF WATER

If your ball is lying in water, you have the choice of playing it from there or picking it out of the water at a loss of one stroke.

One danger of playing from moving water is the possibility of your ball moving while you are swinging down on it. For this reason, I recommend taking the penalty stroke and obtaining a normal lie rather than to chance several futile swings attempting to hit a moving object.

When the ball lies in quiet water, your problem is whether or not the ball is lying too deep in the water to risk playing it. Keeping in mind the false picture the water may give you regarding the ball's position, it might be better here also to accept your penalty stroke and lift the ball out of the water.

If you decide to play the ball anyway, approach the shot as you would a buried sand trap lie. Open the stance and the blade of the club—a No. 9 iron or a sand iron—and strike only slightly behind the ball.

You may have to remove your shoes and socks and wade into the water to take your stance for this shot. But what is that to a golfer intent on saving a stroke!

When the Ball Lies in Casual Water

When the ball is lying in casual water (a temporary accumulation of water not recognized as a permanent part of the hazard) in a trap or water hazard it must be played from where it lies, or lifted under penalty.

If the ball is lying in casual water through the green or on the green, the rules allow you to move the ball to dry ground without penalty but not nearer the hole. The same rule applies when your stance would have to be taken in water through the green or on the green. The ball may be dropped without penalty, but not nearer the hole.

THE GENERAL CONDITIONS
OF TRAP PLAY

No matter how good a golfer you may be; no matter how perfectly you play your shots; no matter how lucky you are in love and cards—sooner or later you will end up in a sand trap.

There are many rules regarding what you can and cannot do when your ball alights in such a hazard, but I'll sum them up like this:

a. In addressing the ball before the shot, the club cannot touch the ground, nor may it make contact on the backward part of the stroke.

b. Any immovable obstacle (branches, grass, etc.) may be touched by the club in the address, backswing or forward swing.

c. Any movable or loose impediment in or touching the hazard *may not* be touched or moved.

d. If the ball is completely covered by sand, only enough may be removed as will enable the player to see the top of the ball.

e. If the swing or stance is interfered with by immovable obstructions, the ball may be lifted and dropped in the trap within two club lengths of the obstructions but not nearer the hole. If the interfering obstacles are movable, they may be moved when interfering with the swing or stance.

The penalties for infractions of the above rules is loss of hole in match play and two strokes in medal play.

HOW TO GET OUT OF DEEP,
DRY SAND

Almost every sand trap shot is made with the clubhead striking the sand behind the ball and then following through with the stroke. The cushion of sand between the clubhead and the ball is necessary to prevent blasting the ball beyond the green.

For a short trap shot (up to 25 feet from the green), the clubhead should strike about two inches behind the ball. The greater the distance required, the closer to the ball the clubhead should strike. However, *never hit closer than one-half inch behind the ball for the explosion shot.*

The swing will vary from an upright motion for a short shot, to a full, normal swing when you want distance from a fairway trap.

In some instances, a long shot from a fairway sand trap can be played much the same as a normal shot from the fairway. This applies only when the lie is perfect and there is no immediate bank to clear. In this case, strike the ball first and then follow through the sand and complete your motion.

Often you will be faced with a shot from a sand trap in which the ball is buried—slightly or almost completely. This need not ruin your game. Play the ball forward a bit toward the left foot and swing the clubhead into the sand a bit nearer to the ball —about an inch to an inch and a half.

You must hit enough behind the ball so that the front edge of the club face gets *underneath* the buried ball. But avoid hitting too far behind the ball or you'll obtain little distance from the stroke.

I like to use the sand iron for such explosion shots, bringing the clubhead from the outside in with an open stance. This all adds backspin to the ball which stops it shortly after it hits the green.

If you need long distance from a half-buried lie in a sand trap, you should close the face of your club slightly to avoid imparting too much height and backspin to the shot. Also avoid the outside-in motion of swinging the clubhead to contact the ball. Employ a normal swing. You might use a club which is less lofted than the sand iron, too, perhaps a No. 6 iron. In difficult cases, however, it is better to settle for a shot merely taking you out of the trap instead of worrying about the distance necessary to make the green.

One very annoying habit of a golf ball when in a sand trap is that of rolling into a heel print left by some thoughtless player. I play this shot as I do any half-buried shot, concentrating on hitting far enough behind the ball to control its distance. If everyone were to observe the etiquette of golf, this shot could be forgotten—smooth out the trap when you're through.

Occasionally, you will be faced with a shot from under the lip of a sand trap. Here you need immediate height to clear the lip of the trap. Otherwise, you are likely to see the ball strike the lip and bounce back into the trap.

The left foot should be planted part of the way up the bank with the knee bent. The right foot thus will have most of the weight on it, and it must be planted firmly in the sand. Play the ball midway between your feet and open the blade of your club.

The arms do most of the work in any short sand trap shot, and they must be firm throughout the stroke. The extent of the backswing and follow-through are determined by the distance of the shot.

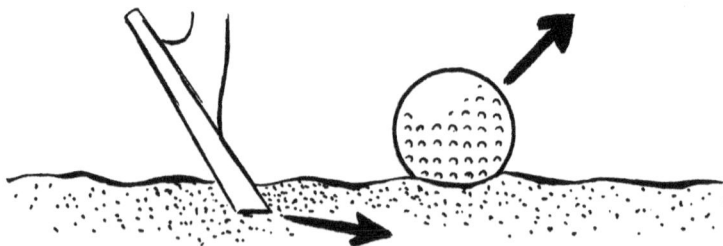

The Explosion Shot

61

PLAYING TRAP SHOTS FROM
WET SAND

When you're shooting from a good lie in a wet sand trap, begin your shot with a firm stance as you did from the dry sand trap. Wiggle your feet around until you get a solid base for the body.

Remember your clubhead will not sweep through wet sand as it does through dry sand. Consequently, be careful not to strike too far behind the ball and sacrifice your power.

Occasionally, the ball can be played from wet sand the same as from a regular fairway lie due to the level, unyielding surface which allows a clear shot at the ball. This is particularly helpful when you are seeking distance from a trap. The swing, of course, is the same as for a normal fairway shot.

Many sand traps are deceptive as to the firmness of the sand. If you cannot examine the traps on a course during practice rounds, or if you are not certain how heavy they may be, you can accurately estimate the texture of the sand when you take your stance. This can be determined by the effort necessary to wiggle your feet into a firm stance.

If the lie is poor in a wet sand trap, you cannot obtain too much distance. Remember, *your main purpose is to get out of the trap in one stroke*. Never take chances on topping the shot in order to gain distance.

However, you can cut down on the immediate height of the shot by playing the ball back toward the right foot. This may add some distance to your shot.

For the shorter explosion out of wet sand, remember to take enough sand but not too much. That may sound like an indefinite statement, but practice is the only method of determining just what a shot like this requires in the amount of sand taken.

PLAYING TRAP SHOTS FROM
VERY SHALLOW OR HARD SAND

When swinging into extremely shallow or hard sand, concentrate on hitting the ball first. You can't use the explosion shot here. If you strike the sand or ground first, this usually will cause the blade of the club to bounce and top the ball.

The shorter the shot, the more upright the swing. For short shots of this type, play the ball back toward the right foot. I would never use an explosion shot from such a surface because striking the sand first will deflect your club face.

The idea of gaining long distance from a poor lie in a fairway trap having this type of surface is purely secondary. First and foremost, you must get the ball out of the sand trap in one shot. Trying for distance in such a situation usually will ruin your chance of escaping the trap.

One method of getting extra distance from this shot is in using a comparatively straight-faced club such as a No. 6 or No. 7 iron. If height is not needed, these clubs can help you obtain distance.

PUTTING OUT OF TRAPS

Practically the only conditions under which a putter should be used out of a sand trap are these:
   a. The ball is perched up in a good lie.
   b. There is no lip or bank between the ball and the green.
   c. The ball need not travel far over sand.

In stroking the ball, use the same method as for a long putt. Don't try to lift the ball or skip it across the sand. Don't chop or cut at the ball. Bring the putter back smoothly and be sure the face of the club hits the ball squarely.

If the conditions call for you to use such a shot don't be ashamed to try it—on occasion the most perfect golf stylists call upon their putter in a trap.

PUTTING IS A BIG PART
OF THE GAME

Putting is one aspect of golf where the small men need not worry about lacking power. Everyone has the ability to become a good putter. And putting is considered from 50% to 80% of anyone's golf game in importance.

The grip differs slightly from the grip in making every other shot in golf. Let the club lay across the palm of the left hand. Close the hand on the shaft and point the thumb down the center of the shaft. The back of the left hand then is square to the hole.

I take a similar grip with the right hand which leaves the palm of that hand square to the hole. The forefinger of my left hand overlaps the little finger of my right hand in a reverse overlap.

This grip, however, is merely one that is comfortable for me. It may not be right for you. The mechanics of successful putting depend a great deal upon what is comfortable and effective for the individual.

I play the ball off my left foot for a normal, level putt. My toes are square to the intended line the putt will travel, and my eyes are directly above the ball. I bring the blade of the putter back slowly, keeping the blade low and square across the line of the putt. I return the blade smoothly, striking the ball at the bottom of the rather flat arc.

Within the past year or so, I have eliminated some of the wrist movement in my putting in favor of a more general movement. My wrists are now firmer on my putts, and the success of my putting has increased considerably.

Another favorite little trick of mine is to sight the line I want the putt to travel. Then, concentrating on the ball's following that line for the first three inches, I stroke the ball. If it follows my intended line for the first three inches, it generally will go in the hole or come mighty close.

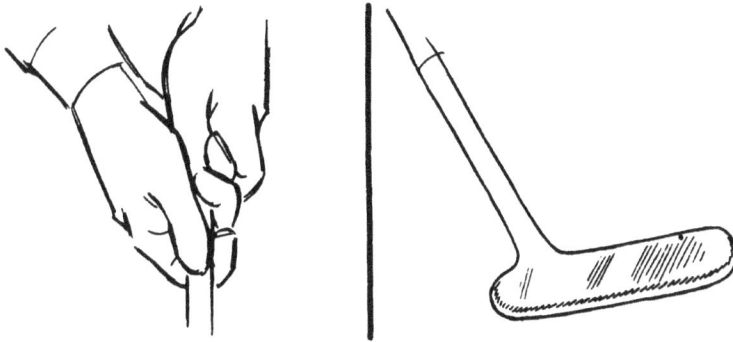

My putting grip and my putter.

I am now using a modified center-shafted putter which I find very successful. In the past I have tried various types of putters and also various styles of putting. Some of my shortcomings on the greens have been publicized quite widely, and they still remain a source of great sorrow to me; they were costly!

I've come mighty close to winning the National Open several times, finishing second on three different occasions. One of the worst cases of my inconsistent putting came in the 1947 National Open at St. Louis. I sank a 20-foot putt on the final hole to tie Lew Worsham for the championship.

In the following day's playoff between Lew and myself, we came to this same 18th hole all even. I was on the green in two strokes, just 15 feet away from the cup, while Lew was just off the green. He chipped up close to the cup, and I was short with my putt, leaving me with a 30½ inch putt. (I know the exact length because the officials measured the distance.)

On the same green where I had rolled in a 20-footer the day before, I blew the 2½-footer that would have kept me in the fight for the championship.

One reason I am putting better today than at any time in my career is I've learned to relax. That's an important feature for successful putting, and I want to emphasize it. If you feel yourself tightening up, just stop things and walk away. Above all, stay loose and relaxed.

Man, Oh man, what a great feeling when your putter is really dropping 'em.

The Putt

GREENS DIFFER GREATLY
IN PLAYING QUALITIES

Because a player is not permitted to test the speed of a green by rolling another ball nor is he allowed to check the grain of the green by scraping the surface, he must become expert in quickly and accurately judging the condition of the putting surface at a glance.

No two greens are exactly alike in playing qualities, and often the same green can be changed considerably in playing qualities in a very short time. Climatic conditions have a great deal of effect on whether a green is fast or slow. Changing the position of the cup on the green can also affect the speed and roll of your putt in addition to changing your method of approaching the green. Uphill, downhill, and sidehill putts all present their own peculiar problems.

What Makes Greens Fast?

A fast green results from several different causes. A dry, hard-packed surface will be a very fast green. If the grass on the green has been closely mowed or recently mowed, you'll be facing a fast green. If you're putting with the grain of the grass, the ball will roll faster. Wind, too, affects putts, although not as greatly as it affects the other shots. When putting under these conditions, your backswing need not be quite as far nor your stroke quite as firm as for a normal putt.

What Makes Greens Slow?

If you're playing golf early in the morning or after a heavy rain, you'll notice the greens will be very slow and soggy. The same applies if the greens have recently been watered. Greens are also slow if the grass is comparatively long. Under any of these conditions, your stroke must be a bit harder and firmer than for a putt on a normal green. Putting against the grain also slows down the ball and must be considered in stroking the putt.

Putting Uphill

The only adjustment I make when putting uphill is to grip the putter a bit more firmly. On every putt I try to give the ball enough power to carry it to the hole and about a foot beyond. This serves to overcome the normal tendency of falling short on an uphill putt.

Putting Downhill

My grip when putting downhill is not as firm as for a normal, level putt. However, *don't hold the club loosely!* If you relax your grip too much, the club will turn in your hand at contact.

Another putting tip to tall players is to use a longer putter if you are more than six feet tall. If you are tall and try to get into a comfortable stance with a regular shafted putter, you may find the position will be cramped and strained.

The opposite will apply if you are exceedingly short—obtain a short-shafted putter.

Putting Over Side-Hill Roll

This is one phase of putting which you must learn for yourself. No one else can help you.

It takes plenty of practice to judge accurately the correct line for a sidehill putt. You must consider the condition and grain of the green along with the slope of the hill.

One thing to avoid in all putts is the tendency to shorten your swing after the ball has been struck. The ball should be hit smoothly, and the motion of the swing carried through to its normal conclusion.

YOUR MENTAL APPROACH TO GOLF

First and foremost, you must have confidence—confidence in your equipment and confidence in your ability to operate it.

Your second mental problem is one of concentration. Consider each shot individually and think it through in advance before you address the ball. Draw a mental image of where you want the ball to go and then eliminate everything else in your mind except how you are going to get the ball to that preferred spot.

Playing for position is a major factor in your mental approach to golf. Figure out just where you want each shot to go. Down the middle of the fairway is not always the best position for your tee shot. On long holes which have "dog-legs" or turns to the right or left, it may be advisable to play your drive toward one or the other side of the fairway.

Always keep in mind the position from which you want to play your next shot. In approaching the green, there is usually one side which is easier and less risky than the other. For instance, the middle may be trapped and the left side open.

Plan your approach shots to the green so you are left with uphill rather than downhill putts. Naturally, the uphill putt is easier and less risky.

Decide in advance whether you should gamble on a shot. Take chances only when you have a reasonable chance of success. For example, if clearing a hazard on your shot is doubtful, why take the risk if it only means playing a six iron shot to the green instead of a five iron shot? The prize is not worth the risk.

In emphasizing concentration, I would like to point out that it is a mental matter, not a physical one. By that I mean you should never concentrate on the shot to the extent that your body becomes rigid or taut. Relaxation is a must in golf, and if you have a tendency to "freeze" when addressing the ball, step back and remind yourself of the necessity of relaxing and start the shot over again. Believe me, I know what I'm talking about here.

CAUSES AND QUICK CURES
FOR COMMON FAULTS

Here are a few ways quickly to check yourself up when a fault suddenly develops in your game. The reason may be found in the list below. But it may well be because of some entirely different error you have fallen into—or a combination of them. So, if the fault persists, don't waste time. Have a pro check your game right away. He'll probably straighten you out in a jiffy.

SHANKING—This is caused by a hurried backswing and downswing and also by forcing extra distance from a club. To avoid this, take your time in swinging, keep your wrists and arms relaxed and don't press the shot. Keep the hands in close to the body on the swing.

PUSHING—Chief reason for pushing a shot is an incorrect stance. The pushed shot travels in a straight line but to the right of the intended line. Check your stance—it may be closed too much. Use a square stance.

PULLING—This is the opposite of pushing. Here, your stance is probably too open.

TOPPING—This aggravating habit comes from several sources. When the golfer tries to scoop the ball into the air with the club, he generally applies body action or wrist action which draws the clubhead out of its intended path. Thus, the club strikes the ball on the upswing, resulting in a topped shot. Don't scoop the ball—let the loft of the club face lift the ball for you.

WHIFFING—When you miss the ball entirely, you probably lifted your head too soon. This is an aggravated case of topping in which you don't even touch the ball. Keep your swing in its smooth pattern and keep your head down and your eye on the ball.

SCUFFING—The common cause for scuffing is an attempt—conscious or otherwise—to scoop the ball up into the air. The result is a striking of the ground behind the ball first and then hitting the ball. The cure is to hit the ball "on the downswing" and let the club face do the lifting.

SLICING—The most common cause of slicing is drawing the clubhead across the ball from the outside in. This is in turn caused by too wide a stance or too weak a left hand. Check your stance before addressing the ball; see that the clubhead is started back inside the line; make certain your left side is completing the turn with the weight shifted to the right leg on the backswing; keep the left hand and arm dominating the backswing and start of the downswing. Check your grip.

HOOKING—A hook is produced when the club face is drawn across the ball from the inside out. Check your grip and stance. Make sure you are not adopting any of the habits of the intentional hook. Open your stance slightly and make sure the left hand is not throwing the club away from the body on the downswing.

SKYING—If you're losing too much distance to height, chances are you're teeing the ball too high or using a club with too shallow a face.

YOU CAN CHOOSE A SET OF CLUBS FROM THIS LIST

A full set of golf clubs which can handle all situations and playing conditions, would include the following:

The driver or No. 1 wood is used for maximum distance from the tee or excellent fairway lies.

The brassie or No. 2 wood will give the average player a shot of about 220 yards.

The spoon or No. 3 wood is good for shots of slightly under 200 yards from the fairway.

The No. 4 wood can be used from poor lies and will supply distances of 175 yards for the average player.

The No. 5 wood is really a special club for the person who is hesitant about using the No. 2 iron. This No. 5 wood will give you distances of 160 yards.

The driving iron is used when accuracy from the tee is a primary requisite, and it will supply distances of 200 yards or slightly more.

The No. 2 iron is used from lies where a wood cannot get at the ball cleanly or extreme accuracy is needed. This club is good for slightly under 200 yards for the general golfer.

The No. 3 iron is used for shots of approximately 170 yards.

The No. 4 iron will usually give you 160 yards distance.

The No. 5 iron is the middle iron of the set and is very versatile. This club is good for shots of about 150 yards or less.

The No. 6 iron is used for distances up to 135 yards.

The No. 7 iron begins the pitching irons and is used from approximately 120 yards or less.

The No. 8 iron will give the average golfer distances up to 100 yards.

The No. 9 iron sees plenty of duty in traps, rough, and other lies less than 100 yards from the green.

The sand iron is used principally in sand traps and rough, but it will serve for fairway approach shots as well as the No. 9 iron.

The putter is used for all putts on the green and sometimes for extremely short approaches from the short grass of the apron.

The pitching niblick is a valuable club for lifting high pitch shots over some obstacle. The club is well lofted and is used from as far away as 120 yards.

Of course you are allowed to carry no more than 14 clubs at a time, but if you have a full set you can pick and choose, according to the course and the playing conditions.

COACHWHIP PUBLICATIONS

COACHWHIPBOOKS.COM

Golf
by
Briggs

www.ingramcontent.com/pod-product-compliance
Lightning Source LLC
Chambersburg PA
CBHW042047090426
42733CB00039B/2658